Savvy

Girls Rock

GIRLS

Star

AMAZING TALES OF

Hollywood's

LEADING LADIES

by Shelley Tougas

Consultant:
Victoria Sturtevant, PhD
Director of Film and Media Studies
The University of Oklahoma
Norman, Oklahoma

CAPSTONE PRESS
a capstone imprint

Savvy Books are published by Capstone Press,
1710 Roe Crest Drive, North Mankato, Minnesota 56003
www.capstonepub.com

Library of Congress Cataloging-in-Publication Data
Tougas, Shelley.
Girls star! : amazing tales of Hollywood's leading ladies / by Shelley Tougas.
pages cm.—(Savvy. Girls rock!)
Summary: "Through narrative stories, explores actresses who have made major contributions in movies and television"—Provided by publisher.
Includes bibliographical references and index.
ISBN 978-1-4765-4057-3 (library binding) — ISBN 978-1-4765-6163-9 (ebook pdf)
1. Actresses—United States—Biography—Juvenile literature. 2. Motion picture actors and actresses—United States—Biography—Juvenile literature. 3. Television actors and actresses—United States—Biography—Juvenile literature. I. Title.
PN2285.T63 2014
791.4302'8092273—dc23
[B]   2013022097

Editorial Credits
Jennifer Besel, editor; Heidi Thompson, designer; Wanda Winch, media researcher;
    Laura Manthe, production specialist

Photo Credits
Corbis: AP/Marion Curtis, 53 (bottom), Bettmann, 56 (left), Douglas Kirkland, 57 (middle), E.J. Camp, 50, Sunset Boulevard, 56 (right), 57 (l), Sygma/Ira Wyman, 26; CriaImages.com/Jay Robert Nash Collection, 6, 7, 10, 37, 46, 54, 55; Getty Images Inc., 42, Alberto E. Rodriguez, 34 (top), Michael Tullberg, 21 (l), Photo Bank/NBCU, 43, Photo Bank/NBCU/NBC/Paul W. Bailey, 12, UNHCR/J Redden, 52, WireImage/Kevin Mazur Archive, 45 (l), WireImage/ Robin Marchant, 23, WireImage/Sgranitz, 32; Globe Photos: Hakim Photos, 4; iStockPhoto Inc: tanebeau, cover, 1; Library of Congress: Prints and Photographs Division, 11, 28, 47, 48, 49, 58, 59; Newscom: Album, 8, 38, UPI/Jim Ruymen, 40 (right), ZOJ Wenn Photos/WP#AMU, 61 (t), Zuma Press/20th Century Fox, 15, Zuma Press/Everett Collection, 21 (right), Zuma Press/Minneapolis Star Tribune, 16, Zuma Press/Nancy Kaszerman, 44 (right), Zuma Press/Richard Lautens, 27, Zuma Press/Tleopold, 34 (b); Shutterstock: Africa Studio, 26 (b), Alexander Lukyanov, 4, 30-31 (floral design), Bariskina, 13, 50-51, 54 (floral design), Darii-s, 9 (background), DeCe, 3, Featureflash, 45 (right), Featureflash/Paul Smith, 19, 20 (l), 24, 39, 60 (b), Featureflash/Steve Vas, 57 (right), Fer Gregory, 62-63, Helga Esteb, 31 (all), 35 (b), Helga Pataki, 10-11 (floral), iadams, 3, 64, Igor Shikov, 34-35 (film strip), Incomible, 6-7 (b), 14-15 (leaf design), Ivan Lord, 46-47 (border), Jaguar PS, 53 (t), 61 (b), Joe Seer, 30, 41 (l), Leskus Tuss, cover, 1 (lights), linagifts, 60-61 (floral element), mart, 56-57 (top), Milen, 55 (floral design), Natalia Hubert, 38 (bl), onime, cover (carpet), pzAxe, 28-29 (background), Rena Schild, 44 (l), s_bukley, 20 (right), 35 (t), 40 (l), 41 (right), 51, 60 (t), ussr, 38 (m), VectorPic, 38 (br), zubarevid, 52-53

Direct quotations are placed within quotation marks and appear on the following pages. Other pieces written in first-person point of view are works of creative nonfiction by the author.
p6: www.biography.com/people/katharine-hepburn-9335828?page=2; p11: www.cmgww.com/stars/monroe/ about/quote_by.html; p15: aaspeechesdb.oscars.org/link/074-3/; p18–19 www.people.com/people/julia_roberts/ biography/0,,20004360,00.html; www.biography.com/people/julia-roberts-9460157; p22: www.imdb.com/name/ nm0001856/bio; p25: www.womenwhochangedamerica.org/profile/tina-fey/; *Bossypants* by Tina Fey (Little, Brown and Co.: New York, 2011. p 145); p29: www.biography.com/people/hattie-mcdaniel-38433; p33: aaspeechesdb.oscars. org/link/057-3/; p44: www.glamamor.com/2012/10/cinema-connection-were-all-tied-up-over.html; online.wsj. com/article/SB10001424052970204425904578072632618320160.html; p45: uk.lifestyle.yahoo.com/jennifer-anistons- hair-evolution-rachel-beach-waves-172756687.html; www.mydaily.co.uk/2011/07/03/sarah-jessica-parker-best- dresses-outfits-fashion/; p47: www.pbs.org/wgbh/amex/pickford/peopleevents/p_pickford.html; p53: www. looktothestars.org/news/9575-betty-whites-91st-birthday-charity-wish; p55: www.queensofvintage.com/bette-davis- vs-joan-crawford/; p56: www.kennedy-center.org/explorer/artists/?entity_id=3814; p57: www.imdb.com/name/ nm0000149/bio; www.rollingstone.com/movies/reviews/beasts-of-southern-wild-20120628

Printed in the United States of America in Brainerd, Minnesota.
092013   007770BANGS14

True Stars

Film unwound from a moving reel, and a bright light shone. The curtains opened. A story began.

And the world has never been the same.

Moving pictures—the movies—redefined entertainment, influenced culture, and gave fans an escape from their lives.

Women conquered the early film world. Then they took modern movies and TV by storm. Stylish. Beautiful. Sassy. Enchanting. Actresses give our favorite movies and shows heat and heart.

Talented actresses invite us to another life, another place, another time. A great actress builds a potent connection with her audience. Together, we laugh, sob, scream, think, wonder, and dream.

Meryl

June 22, 1949–

Meryl Streep counted her money. Nope. Not enough for a hotel.

With no place to go after her theater performance, the young actress curled up in a London park and slept. Across the street was the ultra-expensive Ritz Carlton hotel. She promised herself that someday she'd stay at that fancy hotel.

She didn't break that promise. By the 1970s Streep was gaining attention in her onstage roles. Then in 1977 she broke into film. Soon the theater actress turned into a movie star.

Streep is universally accepted as one of the world's best actresses. She is known for dissolving into her characters. Costars say she prepares for a movie with the intensity of a marathon runner ... times 10.

When Streep played a violinist, she practiced six hours every day for eight weeks. When her character was a chubby housewife, she gained 20 pounds. When she played a Polish Holocaust survivor, she studied both Polish and German languages.

Over more than three decades, Streep has been an Oscar nominee a record-setting 17 times and won three times. She truly is Hollywood's leading lady.

Streep

Reeling Through Streep's Career

1978 – *The Deer Hunter* *

1979 – *Kramer vs. Kramer* **

1981 – *The French Lieutenant's Woman* *

1982 – *Sophie's Choice* **

1983 – *Silkwood* *

1985 – *Out of Africa* *

1986 – *Heartburn*

1987 – *Ironweed* *

1988 – *A Cry in the Dark* *

1990 – *Postcards from the Edge* *

1994 – *The River Wild*

1995 – *Bridges of Madison County* *

1998 – *One True Thing* *

1999 – *Music of the Heart* *

2002 – *Adaptation* *

2002 – *The Hours*

2006 – *The Devil Wears Prada* *

2008 – *Mamma Mia!*

2008 – *Doubt* *

2009 – *Julie and Julia* *

2011 – *The Iron Lady* **

* Nominated for an Oscar   ** Won an Oscar

Katharine HEPBURN

May 12, 1907–June 29, 2003

Katharine Hepburn's pants were missing. They'd vanished, and a skirt was in their place. Hepburn realized her pants had been seized by studio staff. They insisted she wear a skirt. Pants were for men, they said, not for glamorous movie stars. So Hepburn simply walked around the studio, wearing only a shirt and underwear. The pants were quickly returned.

Hepburn was part sass, part class. The movie camera captured her unusual personality, and fans loved her. Hepburn's feisty personality is part of her legend. She didn't wear makeup in public, she wouldn't sign autographs, and she never kept her opinions to herself.

In 1962 Hepburn left her career to care for actor Spencer Tracy, the love of her life. When she returned to film, it was big. She won three of her four Oscars after she was 60 years old. The fearless actress died at age 96. "Life is hard," she once said. "After all, it kills you."

A TIMELINE OF TWO HEPBURNS

Audrey and Katharine Hepburn share a last name and some amazing accomplishments. But, no, they were not related.

Katharine Hepburn   Audrey Hepburn

won the Oscar for *Morning Glory* — **1932**

nominated for *The Philadelphia Story* — **1940**

nominated for *The African Queen* — **1951**

nominated for *Sabrina* — **1954**

1935 — nominated for *Alice Adams*

1942 — nominated for *Woman of the Year*

1953 — won the Oscar for *Roman Holiday*

Audrey HEPBURN

May 4, 1929–January 20, 1993

Audrey Hepburn danced during Germany's takeover of the Netherlands during World War II (1939–1945). She danced through hunger so intense her war-torn family ate tulip bulbs.

But she couldn't dance forever. She'd nearly starved during the war, leaving her too weak to be a great ballerina. After a few movie roles in Europe, she landed a lead role in *Gigi*, a Broadway show. The great reviews made an impression in Hollywood.

Her first Hollywood movie, *Roman Holiday*, brought her only Oscar. Winning Hollywood's biggest award after her first film? Hepburn was something special, and scripts poured in. But acting was only part of her image.

Hepburn redefined fashion. Hollywood's stars boasted curvy, full figures with big hair and over-the-top dresses. Hepburn was tall, pancake thin, and boyish. She daringly cut her hair short and wore capri pants with ballet flats to movie release parties.

Her chic fashion, subtle humor, and dramatic range made her a Hollywood favorite.

nominated for
The Rainmaker

nominated for
Breakfast at Tiffany's

won for *Guess Who's Coming to Dinner*
nominated for *Wait Until Dark*

won the Oscar for
On Golden Pond

1955–1956—1959—1961–1962 — 1967–1968 — 1981

nominated for
Summertime

nominated for
Suddenly, Last Summer
nominated for
The Nun's Story

nominated for
Long Day's Journey into Night

won the Oscar for
The Lion in Winter

Rita Moreno
December 11, 1931–

Rita Moreno is a stunning actress with the rare ability to sing, dance, and act. She's a groundbreaking Latina entertainer. Moreno is one of only 11 people to have earned honors from the four major entertainment awards, also known as the EGOT.

Moreno won Emmy Awards in 1977 and 1978 for her appearances on *The Muppet Show* and *The Rockford Files*.

Moreno won a Grammy Award in 1972 for her work on the soundtrack for the TV show *The Electric Company*.

Moreno won the 1961 Oscar for best supporting actress for her role in *West Side Story*. She became the first Hispanic actress to win the award.

Moreno won the 1975 Tony Award for best featured actress in a play for her work in *The Ritz*.

Marilyn **Monroe**

June 1, 1926–August 5, 1962

The army photographer touring the factory called me beautiful.

Beautiful!

Back then I was nothing special. Just Norma Jeane Baker. A girl raised in foster homes. A girl stuck in a 1940s factory job because the men were fighting the war.

But after that army photographer took my picture, I met other photographers and became a model. As soon as I made money from my pictures, I quit that dirty factory and signed a movie contract. I worked hard to create my image.

I went from brunette to blond.

I went from Norma Jeane to
Marilyn Monroe.

I won roles in movies. *Some Like It Hot* and *Gentlemen Prefer Blondes* were hits. Everyone said I was great in those films. Still, the press and studio big shots treated me like a dumb blond. I liked being Hollywood's beauty, but I wanted to be a serious actress too. I took acting classes and worked hard.

But I never got the respect I deserved, the respect I craved. People complained that I was unreliable. They didn't understand. I had a lot of stress. Three divorces. So much pressure and loneliness. I had no support from the studio, even though I helped build its bank account. "An actress is not a machine," I said, "but they treat you like a machine. A money machine."

Now historians say I was smarter, funnier, and stronger than I got credit for during my life. They say I'm forever an icon.

Forever Marilyn

11

Redheaded
FUNNY FRIENDS

Carol Burnett
April 26, 1933–

Lucille Ball
August 6, 1911–April 26, 1989

My Friend Carol

Carol Burnett stunned the audience. I was at the theater, enjoying a new play, *Once Upon a Mattress*. This unknown actress—Carol—glowed with talent, so I invited myself backstage to meet her. I could tell she was nervous. I told her to give me a call. And she did.

Our friendship started fast as a light switch. We were both raised by grandparents. I understood the pain of missing parents.

Carol's brains gave her a new life. She won a college scholarship and studied drama. I swear she spent more time scouting for parts than she did with her textbooks. But it worked. A funny nightclub bit got her on late-night TV talk shows.

That on-the-spot nightclub humor made her a Broadway powerhouse. Carol had a booming voice, comic timing, and could make a powerful connection with her audiences.

I wanted her on TV. I offered her a show at my production company, not because she was a friend, but because she was that good. Carol passed. She wanted to front her own variety show.

Smart move. *The Carol Burnett Show* ran for 11 years and nabbed 22 Emmys. That woman knew how to build an audience. As part of every show, she'd take questions from the audience. Without fail, she'd be asked to do her famous Tarzan impression. And goodness, could she howl!

As I know too well, comedies age and end. *The Carol Burnett Show* was one of the last musical-sketch comedies on TV. Carol kept working, though, showing some dramatic muscle and winning serious awards. The Presidential Medal of Freedom. Induction into the Academy of Television Arts & Sciences Hall of Fame.

Serious awards for TV's funny woman, my friend Carol Burnett.

My Friend Lucy

Lucille Ball was already a legend when we became friends. Lucy and Carol—two redheaded comedians in a comedy world ruled by men.

Lucy's known for her groundbreaking TV comedy. Fans adored *I Love Lucy*. She played a wacky housewife who was constantly stirring up trouble.

Before Hollywood, Lucy was a struggling nobody like the rest of us. Her father died when she was a toddler. Her strict step-grandparents raised her. I understand why she left at 15. She chased acting jobs, even though she struggled with drama classes. On the road to Hollywood, she wondered if her carrot-top might be holding her back. So she dyed her hair blond. She won small parts in 43 films but still couldn't get a film director's attention.

But redheaded Lucy blossomed on television.

Lucy and I developed a deep friendship after meeting in 1959. It was my second night starring in the play *Once Upon a Mattress*. Nervously I greeted the famous Lucille Ball. Our friendship was born.

My friend Lucy. Such a sweet woman. Each year on my birthday, Lucy sent me flowers. On the morning of my 56th birthday, the radio announced that the legendary Lucille Ball had died. My heart ached. Later that afternoon I got her flowers. Even in Lucy's last hours, she was thinking about me.

I loved Lucy. Everybody did.

Carol Burnett

LENA

Horne

June 30, 1917—May 9, 2010

Lena Horne glared at Hollywood's big shot producers. She told them she would not now, not in the future, not ever play a maid, a nanny, or a waitress.

No actress—especially not an African-American actress—had ever had the guts to make such demands.

But Horne did.

It was the 1940s, and Horne dreamed of leaving her singing career and becoming a movie star. With her light skin, she could pass for a well-tanned white woman. White audiences in New York's club scene accepted her because she looked almost like them.

When a studio rep asked Horne to audition in Hollywood she knew it was her chance at movie stardom.

But she knew she'd need a backbone, not a wishbone.

Hollywood's barriers were bigger and stronger than the club scene. Roles for African-Americans were so limited they could be stored in a folder. But her talent, her beauty, and her light skin opened doors closed to other actors of color.

MGM Studios accepted her terms—no maid, nanny, or waitressing roles. Horne starred in hits such as *Stormy Weather* and *Cabin in the Sky*. Soon she was the highest-paid black actress in Hollywood.

Her acting career came to a screeching halt in 1947. Some members of Congress believed communism was secretly spreading through the country. They accused some of Hollywood's biggest names, including Horne, of being communists.

Horne, known for speaking up and challenging racism, was branded a communist and forbidden by Congress to work in movies or TV. She was forced to return to her singing career until the communist hunt ended.

This Moment is for Lena

When Halle Berry won an Oscar for best actress in 2001, she held the award high and said, "This moment is for Dorothy Dandridge, Lena Horne, Diahann Carroll." Berry had just become the first African-American actress to win an Oscar for her leading role in *Monster's Ball*.

Berry went on to say her Oscar was for "every nameless, faceless woman of color that now has a chance because this door tonight has been opened."

Judy

June 10, 1922–June 22, 1969

I packed big things into a short life. One Oscar, 32 movies, 250 radio gigs, and 1,100 concerts—give or take a few.

Even today's kids know me. I'm the girl tossed by a tornado into the colorful land of Oz. Since 1939 fans of every age can sing "Somewhere Over the Rainbow" or "We're Off to See the Wizard."

I started performing at age 2, so my resume grew faster than I did. My parents had three talented girls. They turned us into a singing act, moved us to California, and by the time I was 14, I was making movies.

Hollywood had a hard time letting me grow up. I had to get married before they would put me in adult roles. I had three marriages, poor health, stress, and trouble with studios. Even though I made money for MGM, studio leaders fired me because I was depressed.

It seems like both success and hard times hit me earlier than most. Before movies, when I was just a child singer, they said I was a little girl with a great big voice. I got the Cecil B. DeMille Award for lifetime achievement when I was 39!

People say my singing, acting, comedy, and all those awards made me a legend. My booming voice. My acting skills. My beauty. And *The Wizard of Oz*, the movie with a life all its own.

My real life wasn't as dramatic or glamorous as it seemed. But I'm lucky to have left a legacy. I'll be remembered by generations to come.

Garland

Julia ROBERTS

October 28, 1967—

Julia Roberts. America's sweetheart. An actress who director Gary Marshall described as "a cross between Audrey Hepburn, Lucille Ball, and Bambi." And in 2000 *Forbes*' magazine called her the most powerful person in the entertainment industry.

Powerful praise for a powerful star.

Roberts moved to New York in 1985 with ambitions as big as her smile. She wanted to be an actor like her older brother Eric. Within five years, she made her star turn in *Pretty Woman*, which earned $463 million worldwide.

She won her first Oscar in 2000 for a movie about Erin Brockovich, a single mom who took down a company for polluting water and making people sick. Roberts also got a $20 million paycheck for that film. At the time, it was the largest payday for a female star.

Roberts is an A-list actress who dominates the box office with both comedies and dramas. And she is one of the world's favorite actresses.

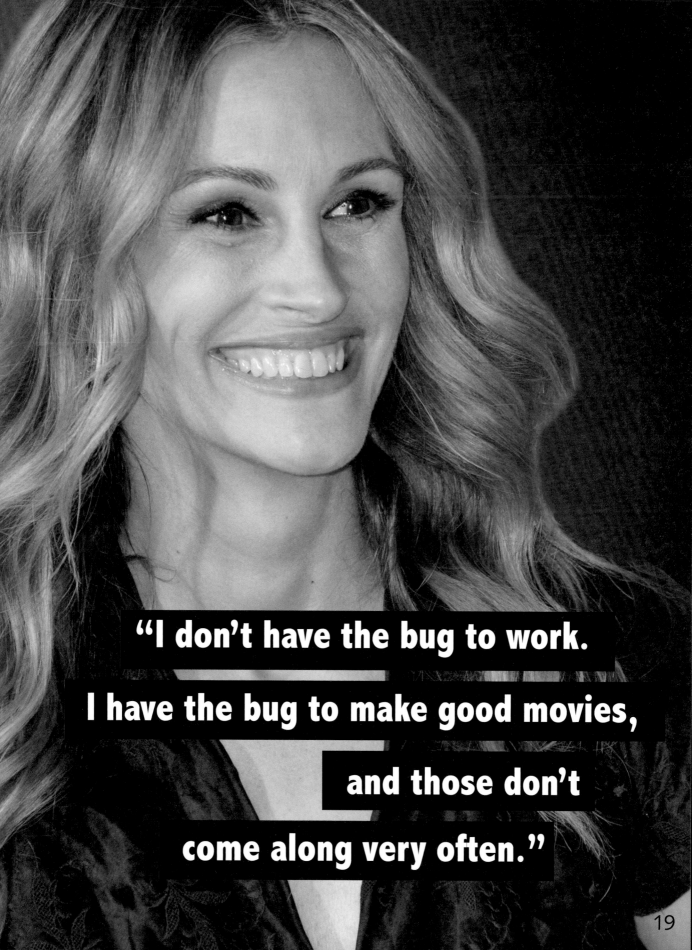

"I don't have the bug to work.

I have the bug to make good movies,

and those don't

come along very often."

Famous Voices

They're more than voices—these women are voice artists. They bring cartoons to life with distinct and often funny vocal performances.

NANCY CARTWRIGHT

October 25, 1957–

For 25 years Nancy Cartwright has been the voice of the 10-year-old bad boy Bart Simpson on *The Simpsons*.

But Cartwright is a master of vocal disguise. Simpsons' viewers probably don't know she also voices other characters on other shows. Just a few of her roles include Chuckie in *Rugrats*, Chip in *The Kellys*, and Rufus in *Kim Possible*.

JUNE FORAY

September 18, 1917–

With a twist of the tongue, June Foray can change her voice from that of a grandmother to one of a young child. The vocal twists never stop.

Foray's career skyrocketed in the 1950s. Her voice was sprinkled into children's records, cartoons, and radio shows. Among them: Granny in *Tweety and Sylvester*, Lucifer in *Cinderella*, Rocky and Natasha in *The Bullwinkle Show*, and Grandma Fa in *Mulan*.

For more than 60 years, Foray has been Hollywood's cartoon queen.

TRESS MACNEILLE

June 20, 1951–

Tress MacNeille acted, studied with a voice coach, and grabbed voice-over work whenever she could find it. Soon, she had a voice-over career with more than 200 credits. She voiced Fang from *Dave the Barbarian*, Dot Warner from *Animaniacs*, and Babs Bunny from *Tiny Toon Adventures*.

Now she's the new Wilma Flintstone and the new Daisy Duck. Playing a talking duck may be the toughest voice job in the industry. It's not easy to speak and quack at the same time.

But Tress MacNeille has proven she can do anything.

MAE QUESTEL

September 13, 1908–January 4, 1998

Mae Questel paved the way for female voice artists like Cartwright, Foray, and MacNeille. Questel was the voice behind hundreds of characters that are still heard today. Possibly her most famous character was 1930s phenomenon Betty Boop. Animators even based many of Boop's physical movements on Questel's actual mannerisms.

Questel lent her voice to a host of other iconic characters, including Olive Oyl on the *Popeye the Sailor* cartoons and Casper, the Friendly Ghost.

Oprah.

Winfrey is her last name, but everyone knows that. Oprah. From the United States to Africa to Japan, Oprah needs no introduction.

A reporting job brought Winfrey to TV. She auditioned for a Chicago talk show and landed the gig. For 25 years, she told people's stories, shined a light on society's issues, made people laugh, and opened minds to diversity.

Winfrey listened. Winfrey understood. Winfrey connected.

She built an entertainment empire, including a magazine, a production company, and an entire cable channel. She's an actress too. Oprah earned a supporting-actress Oscar nomination for the 1985 film *The Color Purple*. Then in 2013 she took on a powerhouse role in *The Butler*.

All that work paid big. After a childhood of poverty, Winfrey became the first African-American woman to make the *Forbes'* billionaires list. These days, she is worth a reported $2.8 billion.

After winning the Daytime Emmy's Lifetime Achievement award, Winfrey withdrew both her name and her talk show from future nominations. She reportedly said, "After you've achieved it for a lifetime, what else is there?"

If there is something else, Winfrey will find it—and conquer it.

Oprah Winfrey
January 29, 1954

TINA FEY

May 18, 1970—

Reporter:

Good afternoon. I'm here with world-class funny lady, Tina Fey. Ms. Fey, when you accepted the 2010 Mark Twain Prize for Humor, you said, and I quote, "Yes, I was the first female head writer at *Saturday Night Live*, and, yes, I was only the second woman ever to be pregnant while on the show. And now ... I am the third female recipient of this prize."

Fey:

Oh, these numbers make me crazy. I'm proud of my work, but I'd rather live in a world where people are no longer counting women's firsts.

Reporter:

How about this description instead? Tina Fey—writer, actor, producer, comedian, the queen of modern comedy.

Fey:

I'm not a queen! I'm a Chicago theater comedian who got a break in 1997 with *Saturday Night Live*. The show opened doors for me. I wrote *Mean Girls* and created *30 Rock*. But I'm not a queen. Not even a princess.

24

Reporter:

Still, people say you broke into the boys' club of comedy. How'd you do it?

Fey:

By being funny.

Reporter:

Some people believe women aren't as funny as men.

Fey:

As I said in my book, *Bossypants*, "Do your thing, and don't care if they like it."

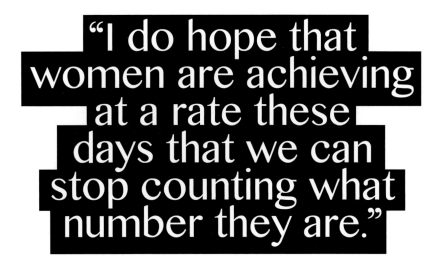

"I do hope that women are achieving at a rate these days that we can stop counting what number they are."

Live From New York!

Amy Poehler said it. Gilda Radner said it. Molly Shannon said it.

"Live from New York, it's Saturday Night!"

For nearly 40 years, *Saturday Night Live* has launched TV, writing, and movie careers for dozens of comedians.

Here are a few of *SNL's* famous female rib-ticklers.

JULIA LOUIS-DREY**F**US

JANE C**U**RTIN

JA**N** HOOKS

KRISTE**N** WIIG

MOLL**Y** SHANNON

GILDA RADNER

LARA**I**NE NEWMAN

CHE**R**I OTERI

JU**L**IA SWEENEY

ANA GA**S**TEYER

Cooking up
Entertainment

Julia Child created the formula for TV cooking shows. Martha Stewart took that formula and whipped up her own show. These two women made kitchen wizardry a steaming success.

August 15, 1912—August 13, 2004

Julia Child's Recipe for Success

INGREDIENTS
a wealthy family
an education at a French cooking school
a chummy, yet ambitious, personality
a dream of bringing the art of French cooking to American kitchens

Julia Child mixed all these ingredients together to create her world-famous cookbook, *Mastering the Art of French Cooking*. Her book's success cooked up the show *The French Chef*, which aired on public television. From 1962 to 1999, Child showed viewers how to prepare French cuisine with fun and flare. She was a master chef and a master at bringing in TV audiences.

August 3, 1941–

Martha Stewart's Recipe for Success

INGREDIENTS
a background in stockbroking
a knack for creative menus and unique presentations
a friendly, yet driven, personality
a dream of turning homemaking into an art

Martha Stewart mixed all these ingredients together to create a media empire the likes of which the world had never seen. Her first book, *Entertaining*, was a bestseller, stirring up more opportunities for Stewart. In 1991 she whipped up the magazine *Martha Stewart Living*, quickly followed by a TV program of the same name. Stewart had trained herself as a cook using Julia Child's *Mastering the Art of French Cooking*. She showed viewers how to prepare delicious and nutritious meals. She also showed audiences how to craft, decorate, and throw perfect parties. She was a master homemaker and a master at bringing in TV audiences.

June 10, 1895–October 26, 1952

HATTIE
McDaniel

Bless you, Hattie McDaniel. My days are full of hauling laundry and scrubbing toilets. I'm a maid, a real-life maid. When I've got more bills than paycheck, I think about Hattie McDaniel standing up for herself and her job.

McDaniel was the first African-American to win an Oscar. And guess what? She got that award in 1939 for playing a maid in *Gone with the Wind*. The National Association for the Advancement of Colored People didn't cheer. They scolded her for taking those kinds of roles.

McDaniel sassed back. "Hell, I'd rather play a maid than be one."

Amen.

Besides, Hollywood was hard enough without that scolding. People there, just like the rest of the country, treated African-Americans like second-class citizens. McDaniel wasn't even invited to the opening of *Gone with the Wind*. Clark Gable, her costar, said if McDaniel wasn't going, then he wasn't going. She quickly got her invitation.

Entertaining was in McDaniel's blood. She could act and sing. At first she made a decent living from radio shows and small movie roles. Directors noticed McDaniel in those small roles. After she stole the show in *The Colonel*, she got plenty of work. Then the Great Depression turned wealthy Americans into poor Americans. Here's a funny fact. McDaniel made more money playing maids than businessmen who used to be rich.

When I mop, scrub, and polish, I think of this amazing woman. Way to go, Hattie McDaniel! Way to go!

No Limits

The old Hollywood featured big drama with glamorous characters just an inch short of perfection. The new Hollywood tries to reflect reality. Many of today's films and TV shows feature people with disabilities—their glamour, their struggles, their everyday lives. These talented actresses inspire the world.

Marlee Matlin

August 24, 1965–

Marlee Matlin is a stunning actress, and she's also legally deaf. Matlin's star moment came when she was cast as a deaf woman in the play *Children of a Lesser God*. Then the play became a movie, and Matlin kept her starring role. Critics praised her ability to show emotion and reveal her character—all without speaking. She won an Oscar for best actress. She was only 20 years old.

Her career jumped to full speed. Matlin did more movies and appeared on TV shows such as *Seinfeld*, *Picket Fences*, *The Practice*, and *The West Wing*. She wrote a children's book and a memoir—and she still finds time to support charities.

Lauren Potter

May 10, 1990–

Lauren Potter is a sassy actress with heart, and she also has Down syndrome. This genetic condition causes learning disabilities and developmental delays.

In real life Potter tried out for the cheerleading squad but didn't make it. But on TV her *Glee* character Becky Jackson made the squad—and became a fan favorite.

Potter taps her fame to advance improvements for people with disabilities. She serves on the Committee for People with Intellectual Disabilities, a group that helps shape national policy at the White House.

Geri Jewell

September 13, 1956–

Geri Jewell is a hilarious actress, and she also has cerebral palsy. This condition makes coordination, including speech and movement, difficult.

Jewell didn't care if her speaking style wasn't perfect. She dreamed of being a stand-up comedian. She first landed a few gigs at Hollywood's Comedy Store. The audience—notorious for being comedy snobs—laughed and applauded.

Quickly, a TV producer snagged her for a part on the show *The Facts of Life*. Jewell became the first person with a disability to win a recurring role in prime time. She later costarred in HBO's critically acclaimed series *Deadwood* during its two-year run.

SALLY Field

November 6, 1946—

Dear Sally,

I've been a fan since 1965, when you first appeared on TV. We were both teenagers then, and it seems like we've grown up together. Marriage, kids, career ups, career downs. As the years passed, I still made time for your movies. Sally, you got better and better.

My father wasn't a fan though. He laughed because I was a fan of your first two TV shows, *Gidget* and *The Flying Nun*. Dad said you'd never break into movies because of those shows. You'd never be taken seriously after playing a nun who could fly!

He was wrong. You won an Emmy for your lead role in the TV movie *Sybil* about a mentally ill woman. Your breakout role. Hollywood's biggest stars had to make room for you. Since then, you've done it all—comedies like *Smokey and the Bandit*, dramas like *Lincoln,* and biographies like *Norma Rae*.

You led the way for other actresses to climb from the small screen to the big screen. You won your first Oscar for *Norma Rae*, and my dad had to admit he was wrong. Sally Field, my favorite actress, does have talent.

When you won your second Oscar for *Places in the Heart*, you held it tight and exclaimed, "And I can't deny the fact that you like me. Right now, you like me!"

Always have, Sally. Always will.

Sincerely,

Your Biggest Fan

Leading *Ladies*

Movies and TV shows don't make themselves. Before the actresses are cast, before the screenwriter delivers the script, before the director yells "action," the film's business arm takes the first step.

Vanessa Morrison

Vanessa Morrison climbed her way from intern to president of Fox Animation Studios. She's the rare executive who's kept her job for 15 years—a lifetime in Hollywood. She's the master of family-friendly movies, including the blockbuster *Ice Age* series.

Today's Hollywood counts Morrison among the company's top business talent.

Bonnie Hammer

The New York Times called Bonnie Hammer "the Queen of Cable." As Chairwoman of NBCUniversal Cable Entertainment Group, she's used the company's deep pockets to buy and build a cable empire. Among her prizes are USA Network and E! Entertainment channel.

Hammer's not the typical executive. She understands stories. She'll work the creative side developing appealing characters, dreaming up plot lines, and finding quality writers. Throughout her career she's revamped both ailing stations and shows.

Amy Pascal

March 25, 1958–

If Bonnie Hammer is the Queen of Cable, then her competitor Amy Pascal is queen of the blockbuster. Pascal is cochairman of Sony Pictures Entertainment. She's responsible for edgy shows such as *Breaking Bad*, thriller films such as *Total Recall*, and science fiction such as *Men in Black*.

In 2012 *Forbes* magazine ranked her number 36 on its list of Powerful Women. Under Pascal's leadership, Sony has had 83 movies open in the top slot since 2000. Measured in numbers or creativity, Pascal is Hollywood's behind-the-scenes superstar.

Anne Sweeney

November 4, 1957–

Anne Sweeney racks up numbers like a calculator—a very big calculator. The ABC/Disney executive's count includes 100 channels and 600 million viewers throughout 169 countries. Three years in a row, *The Hollywood Reporter* ranked her the most powerful woman in show business.

Hollywood's hot shots view Sweeney as a fearless leader who's not threatened by a changing world. Some industry leaders worry digital technology will crush the entertainment business. Not Sweeney. If change is managed, she says, entertainment companies can embrace it. Just provide the shows in ways techies want it—on phones, tablets, or the next big thing.

MARY TYLER
MOORE

December 29, 1936—

Mary Tyler Moore promised to "make it on her own."

And she did. In fact, she started a TV revolution.

Moore first played a typical housewife on a typical 1960s comedy, *The Dick Van Dyke Show*. She won two Emmys for her work on the show. But her big break would come four years after the show ended.

Moore got her own show, billed with her own name. *The Mary Tyler Moore Show* featured the life of 30-something Mary Richards, a character unlike any on TV. Mary Richards was single—not because of divorce or death but by choice. The show's story revolved around Richards' career and friendships. She didn't sit around and sulk about boyfriends.

It was a groundbreaking idea—feminism playing out on TV.

Moore was as smart and daring as the character she played on TV. She knew her popular show wouldn't last forever. So she started a production company that launched some of TV's biggest hits. *The Bob Newhart Show*, *Newhart*, *St. Elsewhere*, and *Hill Street Blues*, came from Moore's company.

On her own,
Mary Tyler
Moore made
it after all.

Dorothy Arzner

January 3, 1897–Oct. 1, 1979

If Hollywood made a movie about Dorothy Arzner, promoters would struggle to capture her incredible life with one title, one description, and one poster.

THE CLUB

Dorothy Arzner wanted to make movies.
They wanted her to type letters.

The astonishing story of Arzner's journey to break Hollywood's great glass ceiling.

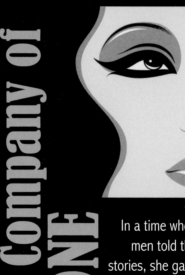

A Company of ONE

In a time when men told the stories, she gave women a voice.

The Director

The camera doesn't tell the story. The person directing the camera does.

The inspiring journey of Hollywood's first female director.

Arzner's career climb is nothing short of remarkable. From typist to screenwriter to film editor, Arzner worked tirelessly to break into the exclusive club of film directors. Arzner transformed 1930s and '40s male-centered films. Her movies featured strong-willed, independent

Michelle Yeoh

August 6, 1962–

Michelle Yeoh is as delicate as a flower and as tough as nails. She's a trained ballerina, and she's known as the "Queen of Martial Arts."

Yeoh was crowned Miss Malaysia in 1983. Soon she was doing commercials with Jackie Chan. Her commercial work led to movie roles. But it was her hard work that really made her shine. Yeoh trained for more than 10 hours a day to get her body into shape for the physical roles she wanted. She did her own stunts, and made a name for herself as Asia's highest-paid female action star.

In 1997 Yeoh made her first American movie, *Tomorrow Never Dies*. Then in 2000 she starred in the box-office smash *Crouching Tiger, Hidden Dragon*.

Yeoh's star continues to climb. She runs her own production company and has continued acting in both Asian and American films.

TV Moms

In TV's early years, the standard rule was that moms stayed home. No hair was out of place. They cleaned the house wearing pearls and high heels.

Then came the '80s. Actresses injected reality into TV. Their characters worked outside the home and juggled family life—often with a dose of grumpy. These "real" moms changed TV forever.

Roseanne Barr

November 3, 1952–

Barr's sitcom *Roseanne* ran from 1988 to 1997. She played Roseanne Connor, a wise-cracking working-class mom. The show often showcased her imperfections as a mother and wife, and fans found a character they could relate to.

Candice Bergen

May 9, 1946–

Murphy Brown ran from 1988 to 1998. Bergen played Murphy Brown, a tough single woman whose career in investigative journalism drove her lifestyle. Bergen's character challenged the belief that single moms ruined family values.

Phylicia Rashad

June 19, 1948–

The Cosby Show ran from 1984 to 1992. Rashad played Claire Huxtable, a distinguished attorney and a wise, loving mom. *The Cosby Show* broke free from a world of stereotyped African-American characters. The show featured a functional family whose mom was brilliant and successful.

Katey Sagal

January 19, 1954–

Married with Children ran from 1987 to 1997. Sagal played Peg Bundy, a homemaker full of attitude. The show's humor was so daring, dark, and over-the-top, many people campaigned to get the show off the air. But the banning campaign turned the show into a hit, and Sagal's character of an almost unfit mother made history.

Elizabeth
TAYLOR

February 27, 1932–March 23, 2011

I kissed her because the script said to kiss her. But from that moment on, I never wanted to leave her side. Elizabeth Taylor and Richard Burton. Our relationship made headlines. But she didn't need me to make the news.

Journalists called her "the last real movie star." Elizabeth Taylor, the woman with lavender eyes. Striking, irresistible, mysterious, clever.

In Hollywood's Golden Age of the 1940s, movies were Americans' entertainment of choice. The industry's legends were born. The 1950s brought change. Americans had TVs. They didn't need to flock to theaters for a good show. Elizabeth's career peaked as the Golden Age waned.

A star since childhood, Elizabeth had movie star glamour and class. In my opinion she's the only actress who could play Cleopatra, history's most enchanting woman. With that role Elizabeth became the first actress to make $1 million for a single film.

Elizabeth and I fell in love making that movie.

Taylor and Burton in 1966

Money and talent. Hollywood blessed her with both. Elizabeth won Oscars for *BUtterfield 8* and *Who's Afraid of Virginia Woolf?*.

But she had her problems—her health, her weight, lavish spending, eight marriages. I had my problems too. That's why we divorced, not once but twice. Problems didn't erase her compassion. She raised money for AIDS research, one of the first celebrities to embrace the cause.

MY DARLING ELIZABETH
THE LAST OF THE GREAT ONES

Acting
Fashionable

Hollywood wardrobes give celebrity watchers something to talk about. Some actresses are their own designers, mixing, matching, and creating a unique style. They're not just actresses. They're trendsetters.

Diane Keaton

January 5, 1946–

Style: a tomboy approach, including tweeds, khakis, dress shirts, and the occasional tie. She also turned accessories like gloves and hats into hip essentials.

Backstory: Keaton nabbed a role the movie *Annie Hall*. She gained status as a style stunner in that film and built a career as an A-list actress. Her style has changed little over the years, except for its influence, which continues to grow.

Review: "She showed such vision ... simultaneously drawing from the past while also being ahead of the trend. There was a seismic shift in fashion when *Annie Hall* hit the movie theaters in 1977. It was a revolution ... from the runways to the street." — *GlamAmor*

Ashley and Mary-Kate Olsen

June 13, 1986–

Style: lavish but not brassy, boutique meets thrift store. Big sunglasses, big jewelry.

Backstory: The twin actresses shared a role in the TV series *Full House*. They made straight-to-DVD movies for girls, then took a break for college. They didn't graduate. Instead, they launched a hit fashion line.

Review: "... their unfussy, elegant collections are so relentlessly not about trend or fashion or red-carpet moments that they've already achieved near-cult status." —*The Wall Street Journal*

Jennifer Aniston

February 11, 1969–

Style: a bouncy, layered haircut with side-brushed bangs. Named "the Rachel," after the character she played on the sitcom *Friends*.

Backstory: *Friends* gave Aniston her breakout role. The show ended in 2004 after 10 years. While on the show, Aniston developed a huge fan following, and her hairstyle became a major 1990s trend.

Review: "Jennifer Aniston will go down in history as the best-tressed star in Hollywood. 'The Rachel,' the '90s bouncy bob she sported in the first two seasons of *Friends*, is one of the most copied hairstyles of all time." — Yahoo! Lifestyle

Sarah Jessica Parker

March 25, 1965–

Style: Carrie, whom Parker played on the show *Sex and the City*, was a shoe fanatic who spent her paychecks on the best footwear. Off screen, Parker boldly experiments with fun shoes, ballerina-style dresses, broaches, and offbeat combinations.

Backstory: Parker was a child actress whose first TV role was a nerd on *Square Pegs*. Her career includes dozens of movies, but her stardom and her trendsetting ways went from big to bigger with her role on *Sex and the City*.

Review: "When Sarah Jessica Parker gets her fashion on, she really gets her fashion on. Okay, so her style icon status might be baffling to some, but to fashionistas, fans and designers she's an inspirational figure with a true understanding of the art of style."
—*My Daily*

October 22, 1844–March 26, 1923

Sarah Bernhardt

Stage actress Sarah Bernhardt's temper boiled. Another actress had insulted her sister. Faster than a blink, Bernhardt slapped that actress across the face. Bernhardt was promptly fired.

Eventually, Bernhardt—born Henriette-Rosine Bernard—would be called the world's greatest actress. But her early years brought no praise. Maybe it's because Bernhardt wanted to be a nun, a lost dream when her mother sent her to acting school. Maybe her quirks affected her performance. At age 15, she bought a coffin and occasionally slept in it.

Bernhardt signed with Odéon Theatre in 1866, worked hard, and finally won critical acclaim in France. When the theater company toured internationally, praise followed. In an era without entertainment reporting or the Internet, Bernhardt accomplished the unimaginable—she became the world's most acclaimed and successful star.

When moving pictures—movies with no sound—became a reality, Bernhardt decided to test the new technology. *Camille*, her third film, was a hit.

Her style, publicized antics, and her genuine talent made Bernhardt more than an actress. She was the first personality of modern entertainment. Her intrigue fueled her fame.

Mary Pickford

April 8, 1892—May 29, 1979

Among Pickford's classics are *Poor Little Rich Girl*, *Pollyanna*, and *Coquette*, for which she won an Oscar. Already a well-known stage actress, Pickford was one of the first actresses to star in silent films and immediately drew crowds of devoted fans.

Advice to Aspiring Actresses

From Mary Pickford, the world's first movie star

1. Allow the lean years to feed your ambition. Hunger motivates. My widowed mother had six kids. I started acting in theater when I was 6 years old to feed our family.

2. Kick and scream. I was determined to audition for theater producer David Belasco. The secretary turned me away. For weeks, I went to his office demanding an audition. No, no, no. Finally, I made a scene. "My life depends on seeing Mr. Belasco!" I got the audition—and the role.

3. Change, then change more. The first change I made was my name. I went from Gladys Marie Smith to Mary Pickford. Then I left theater for the new, silent moving pictures. I had to change my acting. Big gestures in film looked silly. Emotion came from my eyes. Then I changed again from silent pictures to talkies, movies with sound.

4. Work hard. I made 51 films in one year, 236 over my career.

5. Work for yourself. I demanded big salaries and got them. After my hit *Cinderella*, my pay jumped to $10,000 a week. I demanded creative control and got it. I helped form Hollywood's first studio, United Artists Pictures.

November 12, 1929–September 14, 1982

GRACE

Before Grace Kelly was a princess, she was Hollywood's golden girl. In five years Kelly made 11 films, earned one Oscar, and sang a song that became a gold record.

KELLY

In the 1950s Kelly worked with legendary filmmaker Alfred Hitchcock. Hitchcock was known as the "master of suspense," and his films had complex characters and terrifying plots. Kelly starred in three Hitchcock films, playing the perfect blond beauty who had troubles of her own.

But it was Kelly's performance in *The Country Girl* that solidified her place in movie history. She gave a deep, raw performance as the wife of an alcoholic. This role was different from the beauties she played in Hitchcock's films. She won an Academy Award for the role in 1954.

By 1956 Kelly was one of the most respected and highest-paid actresses in the world. But she exchanged the bright lights of Hollywood for the golden sparkle of a crown. She married Prince Rainier III of Monaco and never made another film.

Ingrid Bergman

August 29, 1915–August 29, 1982

Ingrid Bergman was a Hollywood favorite in the 1940s, complete with an Oscar win. She could play characters so naturally it seemed as though she wasn't acting. Her most famous role, as Ilsa in *Casablanca*, showcased her ability to build tension with slight movements and expressions.

Fans loved her acting. They loved her wholesome image too. To the outside world it looked like Bergman had the perfect home life.

But looks can be deceiving.

Bergman's complicated private life nearly ruined her career. She left her husband for Italian director Roberto Rossellini. Fans were stunned, and a U.S. Senator actually scolded her on the Senate floor. Bergman fled to Italy and filmed movies with Rossellini for five years.

She returned to the United States in 1959. Times had changed. Attitudes had changed. Divorce was more acceptable to Americans. Bergman's first U.S. movie in years, *Anastasia*, earned big bucks and awards. From that moment her Hollywood career returned to full speed.

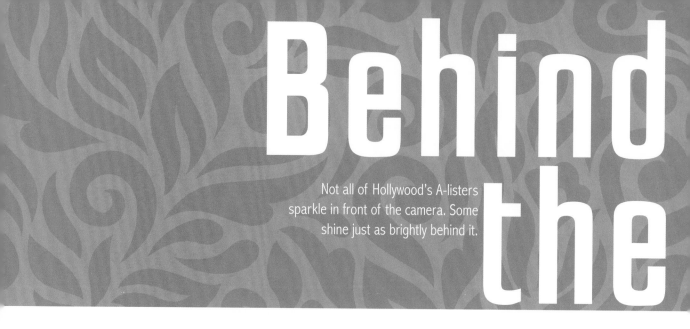

Behind the

Not all of Hollywood's A-listers sparkle in front of the camera. Some shine just as brightly behind it.

Penny Marshall

October 15, 1943—

Penny Marshall held back excitement as she waited to shoot her first commercial. A shampoo commercial! Her costar, a beautiful woman with dazzling blond hair, waited too.

Then Marshall saw the set's two signs.

Pretty Girl.

Ugly Girl.

Marshall knew she wasn't the pretty girl. Still, she was funny and she could act. She auditioned all over Hollywood and won small roles. She joined a TV comedy called *Laverne and Shirley* and became a household name.

Then her career took a right turn. She jumped behind the camera and became a director.

Her second movie, *Big*, a 1988 hit starring Tom Hanks, put her on the A-list. She became the first woman to direct a movie that made more than $100 million in the United States. The great work kept coming. *Awakenings* won an Oscar nomination. *A League of Their Own* earned $100 million and a cult following.

Marshall's directing skills are anything but ugly.

Screen

Nora Ephron

May 19, 1941–June 26, 2012

Nora Ephron is the mother of the modern romantic comedy. She wrote everything from plays to books to blogs, but her laugh-and-love movies made her a screenwriting superstar. Her scripts set the standard for the romantic comedy. Her female characters were strong and independent. They showed a soft side, but they also mastered the smack down.

Actors liked her scripts so much they followed her from movie to movie. Meg Ryan starred in Ephron's *You've Got Mail*, *When Harry Met Sally*, and *Sleepless in Seattle*. Tom Hanks snatched roles in two of those films.

But Ephron, a three-time Oscar nominee, is also remembered for her dramatic work. Like her comedies, actors didn't simply sign onto Ephron's dramatic films. They signed onto Ephron. Meryl Streep starred in both *Silkwood* and *Heartburn*.

Streep landed one more Ephron film before the writer died in 2012. Ephron's last movie, *Julie and Julia*, about the legendary Julia Child, gave Streep her 16th Oscar nomination.

The Act of CHARITY

On screen these actresses fall in love, dodge bullets, and stumble into hilarious situations. In their real lives, they fight real problems around the world.

Angelina Jolie

June 4, 1975–

In 2004 Angelina Jolie toured a Cambodian hospital that mostly treated children with AIDS. Sickened by the lack of care and medicine, she founded the Maddox Center for Children. The center provides education and medicine for kids infected with the deadly virus.

Jolie is also a Special Envoy for the United Nations (UN). With the UN, Jolie works with lawmakers to find ways to help refugees.

Natalie Portman

Natalie Portman is an ambassador and champion for the Foundation for International Community Assistance. Portman supports the group's mission to help women in poor countries. It provides loans for women to start small businesses so they can support their children.

June 9, 1981–

Betty White

January 17, 1922–

When Betty White turned 91, she asked the public for one birthday present. "… please help me raise $10,000 for Morris Animal Foundation." White has worked with the organization for 40 years—almost half her life. The group does research to improve the health of animals.

Definitely N

Bette Davis and Joan Crawford were powerhouse actresses throughout the 1930s and '40s. Both women were Oscar-winning stars. Even though there was plenty of room for both in Hollywood's limelight, the two could not get along.

Hollywood insiders claim the war started over a man. Davis fell for Franchot Tone, her costar in the 1935 film *Dangerous*. But Crawford wanted him too. She not only lured him from Davis, she married him. The war of words began.

Dear Joan,

I hope this letter finds you ~~in a~~ well.

I've read critics are noticing your ~~terrible~~ acting in our film *Whatever Happened to Baby Jane*. And rightly so. You've certainly grown ~~fat and ugly~~ personally and professionally since your first big movie, *Our Dancing Daughters*. Such a ~~childish~~ performance! It's amazing you were just a ~~clumsy~~ teenager when you started dancing in nightclubs with ~~unrealistic~~ dreams of stardom. What a mix of ~~undeserved~~ luck and ~~fake~~ talent!

Joan, some say you're angry because of the ~~violent~~ incident while filming *What Happened to Baby Jane*. I simply tripped. My foot accidentally made ~~brutal~~ contact with your face. Silly me! I'm ~~not~~ sickened when I think about these ~~true~~ reports.

I hope to see you ~~fall flat on your face~~ soon.

Sincerely,
Bette

Bette Davis
April 5, 1908–October 6, 1989

Nearly 30 years later, the actresses agreed to work together in *Whatever Happened to Baby Jane*. The meaty roles could revive both of their careers. Still, they battled throughout filming.

Crawford died in 1977. Even then, the battle continued. Davis said, "You should never say bad things about the dead, only good [things]. Joan Crawford is dead. Good."

Dear Bette,

Thank you for your ~~ridiculous~~ letter.

I hear that newspapers are printing stories about your ~~horrible~~ movies. Reporters are saying you display ~~outrageous~~ attitude, ~~overrated~~ talent, and ~~inappropriate~~ humor. I couldn't ~~dis~~agree more.

Remember when you weren't getting offered any roles? You took out that job wanted ad in the newspaper! Oh, Bette, you are gutsy! That's why people call you Hollywood's ~~dumbest~~ star.

It's nice to share stories about our humble beginnings, especially your ~~awful~~ Broadway career. You had a ~~lackluster~~ work ethic. Fourteen ~~terrible~~ movies in three ~~talentless~~ years! *Of Human Bondage*, *Jezebel*, and *The Petrified Forest* are among history's ~~worst~~ films. Your awards collection is a result of ~~bribing~~ the voters.

Best of luck in your ~~dead~~ career!

Sincerely,
Joan

Joan Crawford
March 23, 1905–May 10, 1977

55

CHILD

Cute, funny, energetic, unique. Movie producers know what they want in child actors. The most important quality? The kids have to love the camera, and the camera has to love them.

Discovered! a young cutie who didn't fear an "alien" costar

Barrymore was adored in the Oscar-winning *ET: The Extra Terrestrial*. She grew into one of Hollywood's romantic comedy princesses.

Barrymore also grew into one of Hollywood's most respected producers. In 1995 she started her own production company, Flower Films, and later produced blockbuster hits such as *Charlie's Angels*.

Shirley Temple

April 23, 1928–

Discovered! a lovable preschooler with curly hair who could sing and dance

Temple made 40 movies, including *Bright Eyes*, a movie tailored just for her. She came in number 18 on the American Film Institute's list of greatest female screen legends.

"As long as our country has Shirley Temple, we will be all right."
—President Franklin Roosevelt

Drew Barrymore

February 22, 1975–

STARS

Jodie Foster

November 19, 1962–

Quvenzhané Wallis

August 28, 2003–

Discovered! a misunderstood, quirky teenager with offbeat style

Ringwald was Hollywood's Teen Queen in the 1980s with blockbusters including *Sixteen Candles*, *Pretty in Pink*, and *The Breakfast Club*.

Molly Ringwald

February 18, 1968–

Discovered! a smart, fearless girl who can play a troubled teen without being one

Foster went from child star to Hollywood powerhouse, winning Oscars for *Silence of the Lambs* and *The Accused*. She's also a Yale graduate and a film director.

Discovered! a young girl, fearless yet innocent

Wallis became the youngest ever Oscar nominee for her role in *Beasts of the Southern Wild*. She was just 9 years old when she was nominated.

"There's no way you won't be captivated by [Quvenzhané] Wallis, chosen ahead of 3,500 candidates to play the tiny folk hero who narrates the story. Her performance in this deceptively small film is a towering achievement."
—*Rolling Stone*

Greta GARBO

September 18, 1905–April 15, 1990

Born into a poor Swedish family, Garbo felt lucky to find work at a department store. Managers noted her beauty and turned her into a store model and star of their commercials. Garbo saw career potential, so she enrolled in drama school. She left the school in 1923, and within two years, she was Europe's top actress.

Then Hollywood called, and she answered. Her thick Swedish accent wasn't a problem. Movies didn't have sound. Her mysterious look and talent for showing emotion made her the perfect silent film star. She shot to international stardom after three Hollywood hits, *The Torrent*, *The Temptress*, and *Flesh and the Devil*.

In the 1930s two things happened. Garbo became one of the world's highest-paid women, and the popularity of movies with sound boomed. Despite her thick accent, Garbo was among the handful of stars who successfully leaped to the talkies. She made 13 more films.

But then she abruptly retired. The way Garbo vanished from the screen only heightened public curiosity about their favorite mystery.

A SILENT STAR

Garbo was an intensely private woman. She feared strangers. She didn't attend her film premieres. She refused to give interviews or autographs.

Historians can only guess why such a private woman would work in movies. When she started acting, she didn't have to speak because movies were silent. Perhaps she never envisioned becoming a star.

Sophia Loren

September 20, 1934–

Sophia Loren lived her mother Romilda's dream. Romilda's strict Italian family had denied her dream to be an actress. So she devoted herself to making Loren a star.

Romilda tracked beauty contests and signed up the teenage Loren. On stage Loren instinctively knew how to turn on the "wow" factor. European filmmaker Carlo Ponte saw a star in the making. She landed a contract to make 10 films in Europe. After *The Gold of Naples* in 1954, she was an Italian superstar headed to Hollywood.

Loren charmed American audiences. Critics noted how she effortlessly shifted from comedy to drama. Then there was her exotic accent, her full figure, and those catlike shimmering eyes. The popular actress jumped between Italian and American movies without losing fans in either country.

More than 50 years after those beauty contests, Loren was still acting. She costarred in 1995's *Grumpier Old Men* and 2009's *Nine*.

Loren's beauty seems untouched by age and so does her talent.

The Bold and the

Damsels in distress. Ruthless rivals. Clueless cuties. Vile vixens. Known as boot camp, soap operas have prepared many Hollywood actresses for the A-list.

Demi Moore

For two years Demi Moore played the tough journalist Jackie Templeton on *General Hospital*. Jackie arrived in Port Charles to save her hypnotized sister and left for bigger adventures after romance failed. Moore's post-soap career highlights:

- box office gold in 1985's *St. Elmo's Fire*

- first actress to earn a $10 million paycheck

- a Golden Globe for the tearjerker *Ghost*.

November 11, 1962–

Susan Lucci

All My Children's Erica Kane had 41 years to cause trouble. Susan Lucci portrayed Erica in every possible mess—from drug addiction to kidnapping to nine marriages.

ABC canceled the show, but Lucci remains soaps' biggest diva.

- 18 Emmy nominations without a single win. Nomination 19 lifted the "Lucci Curse" when she finally got the award.

- wrote a memoir, *All My Life*

December 23, 1946–

Beautiful

Alison Sweeney

September 19, 1976–

Days of Our Lives' fans love to hate Samantha Brady. For 20 years actress Alison Sweeney has played the crisis-magnet Sami. Her worst moments include blackmail, kidnapping, murder, and fake amnesia victim. Sweeney may also be soap's busiest star.

- host of *The Biggest Loser* since 2007
- directs online series *In Tune*
- wrote a memoir *All the Days of My Life (So Far)*

Julianne Moore

December 3, 1960–

Julianne Moore developed her acting chops on *As the World Turns*. Her three-year stint playing Frannie Hughes and her identical sister Sabrina was an acting challenge that prepared her for later movie roles. Today Moore is one of the most respected actresses of her generation.

- won a Daytime Emmy
- four Oscar nominations, including two in 2002 for both best actress in a leading role and best actress in a supporting role
- listed among *Entertainment Weekly*'s Greatest Actresses of the 1990s

So many stars got their start on soaps. Here are just a few more.

Cicely Tyson—*The Guiding Light*

Eva Longoria—*The Young and the Restless*

Kelly Ripa—*All My Children*

Marisa Tomei—*As the World Turns*

Meg Ryan—*As the World Turns*

Phylicia Rashad—*One Life to Live*

Sarah Michelle Gellar—*All My Children*

Susan Sarandon—*A World Apart*

Girls Shine!

From silent films to modern-day TV and blockbusters, women have cast magic and changed lives. They broke stereotypes and pushed the industry in new directions.

Hollywood's leading ladies truly lead.

They tell stories.

They crunch numbers.

They write scripts.

They direct action.

They control entire studios.

They make us laugh, think, and feel.

And they prove that girls shine.

All of these women have displayed spectacular talent over several decades. Their placement on the timeline reflects the decade in which they truly rose to fame in their Hollywood careers.

1900s: Sarah Bernhardt

1910s: Mary Pickford

1920s: Greta Garbo

1930s: Bette Davis
Dorothy Arzner
Hattie McDaniel
Joan Crawford
Judy Garland
Katharine Hepburn
Mae Questel
Shirley Temple

1940s: Ingrid Bergman
June Foray
Lena Horne

1950s: Audrey Hepburn
Grace Kelly
Lucille Ball
Marilyn Monroe
Sophia Loren

1960s: Carol Burnett
Elizabeth Taylor
Julia Child
Rita Moreno

1970s: Betty White
Diane Keaton
Mary Tyler Moore
Meryl Streep
Penny Marshall
Sally Field

1980s: Candice Bergen
Demi Moore
Drew Barrymore
Geri Jewell
Jodie Foster
Katey Sagal
Marlee Matlin
Molly Ringwald
Nancy Cartwright
Nora Ephron
Oprah Winfrey
Phylicia Rashad
Roseanne Barr

1990s: Alison Sweeney
Angelina Jolie
Ashley Olsen
Jennifer Aniston
Julianne Moore
Julia Roberts
Martha Stewart
Mary-Kate Olsen
Michelle Yeoh
Sarah Jessica Parker
Susan Lucci
Tina Fey
Tress MacNeille

2000s: Amy Pascal
Anne Sweeney
Bonnie Hammer
Halle Berry
Natalie Portman
Vanessa Morrison

2010s: Lauren Potter
Quvenzhané Wallis

Index

Aniston, Jennifer, 45, 63
Arzner, Dorothy, 38, 63

Ball, Lucille, 12–13, 63
Barr, Roseanne, 40, 63
Barrymore, Drew, 56, 63
Bergen, Candice, 40, 63
Bergman, Ingrid, 49, 63
Bernhardt, Sarah, 46, 63
Berry, Halle, 15, 63
Burnett, Carol, 12–13, 63

Cartwright, Nancy, 20, 21, 63
Child, Julia, 26, 27, 63
Crawford, Joan, 54–55, 63

Davis, Bette, 54–55, 63

Ephron, Nora, 51, 63

Fey, Tina, 24–25, 63
Field, Sally, 33, 63
Foray, June, 20, 21, 63
Foster, Jodie, 57, 63

Garbo, Greta, 58, 63
Garland, Judy, 16–17, 63

Hammer, Bonnie, 34, 35, 63
Hepburn, Audrey, 6–7, 63
Hepburn, Katharine, 6–7, 63
Horne, Lena, 14–15, 63

Jewell, Geri, 31, 63
Jolie, Angelina, 52, 63

Keaton, Diane, 44, 63
Kelly, Grace, 48, 63

Loren, Sophia, 59, 63
Lucci, Susan, 60, 63

MacNeille, Tress, 21, 63
Marshall, Penny, 50, 63
Matlin, Marlee, 30, 63
McDaniel, Hattie, 28–29, 63
Monroe, Marilyn, 10–11, 63
Moore, Demi, 60, 63
Moore, Julianne, 61, 63
Moore, Mary Tyler, 36–37, 63
Moreno, Rita, 8–9, 63
Morrison, Vanessa, 34, 63

Olsen, Ashley, 44, 63
Olsen, Mary-Kate, 44, 63

Parker, Sarah Jessica, 45, 63
Pascal, Amy, 35, 63
Pickford, Mary, 47, 63
Portman, Natalie, 53, 63
Potter, Lauren, 30, 63

Questel, Mae, 21, 63

Rashad, Phylicia, 41, 63
Ringwald, Molly, 57, 63
Roberts, Julia, 18–19, 63

Sagal, Katey, 41, 63
Stewart, Martha, 27, 63
Streep, Meryl, 4–5, 51, 63
Sweeney, Alison, 61, 63
Sweeney, Anne, 35, 63

Taylor, Elizabeth, 42–43, 63
Temple, Shirley, 56, 63

Wallis, Quvenzhané, 57, 63
White, Betty, 53, 63
Winfrey, Oprah, 22–23, 63

Yeoh, Michelle, 39, 63

Read More

McCann, Michelle Roehm and Amelie Welden. *Girls Who Rocked the World*. New York: Alladin, 2012.

Schwartz, Heather E. *Girls Rebel! Amazing Tales of Women Who Broke the Mold*. Girls Rock! North Mankato, Minn.: Capstone Press, 2014.